1st Edition October 2022

If you find an error in this book, please email support@quovadimusmedia.co.uk, with a description of the error and the page number.

About Quo Vadimus Media Ltd

We are a learning & media company based in the United Kingdom, using evidence-informed practice to help individuals and businesses to learn and improve in a changing world. We bring a wealth of knowledge from schools, colleges, universities, and academic research to improve learning.

Our services and products are based on and developed from over 25 years of experience in the self-improvement and education sectors.

We provide online learning as well as producing print & digital publications to enhance learning and retention of knowledge.

Website: https://quovadimusmedia.co.uk

About the Author

Graeme Lamb is the founding Director of Quo Vadimus Media Ltd, a lecturer in accountancy in a college of Further Education in the northwest of England, and a practising bookkeeper holding AATQB (qualified bookkeeper) status with the AAT.

About this Book

This book is a series of questions based around the key topics for the AAT L2 Q2022 unit, Principles of Bookkeeping Controls. The questions are identical to those in the Principles of Bookkeeping Controls Study Guide, published by Quo Vadimus Media Ltd.

This book is aimed at:

- Students who have not bought the study guide but would welcome more practice questions and answers.
- Students who have purchased the Kindle edition and would welcome a more accessible version of the questions and answers.
- Students who have purchased the print edition and would welcome a more accessible version of the questions and answers.

Skills & Knowledge Tests - Chapter 1

QUESTION 1

For each of the payment methods listed below, identify how long it will take for the transaction to be deducted from the bank account balance.

Method	Same Day	Next Day	At a later date when bill is paid
Cheque			
Bank Draft			
CHAPS			
Cash			
Credit card			
Standing order			
Direct debit			
Faster Payments			
BACS			
Debit card			

QUESTION 2

For the following potential uses, match the transaction with the payment method. In your answer, enter the relevant number.

1 – a large purchase, e.g., property.

2 – expenses for travelling members of staff, e.g., salespersons.

3 – for buying tea and coffee from a local corner shop.

4 – purchase of a ream of printer paper online.

5 – paying a bill by post.

6 – buying a vehicle for the business.

7 – monthly payments of the same amount.

8 – monthly payments of varying amounts.

9 – payment of wages.

10 – paying a contractor's bill online.

Method	Potential purchase/expense
Cheque	
Bank draft	
CHAPS	
Cash	
Credit card	
Standing order	
Direct debit	
Faster payments	
BACS	
Debit card	

QUESTION 3

Highlight each of the following actions that will improve the solvency of a business, by either keeping cash in the business for longer or by maximising the speed of incoming cash.

Action	Will improve solvency
Pay by cheque whenever possible	
Encourage customers to pay by cheque	
Pay suppliers as soon as possible	
Pay suppliers as late as possible (within the terms)	
Encourage customers to pay as late as possible (within the terms)	
Encourage customers to pay as soon as possible by offering discounts	

QUESTION 4

The balance of the bank account on the bank statement is £4,522 CR. The Cash Book shows unpresented cheques of £980 and outstanding lodgements of £1,210. Assuming all other transactions are present, what is the balance of the Cash Book?

QUESTION 5

The balance of the bank account on the bank statement is £466 DR. The Cash Book shows unpresented cheques of £234 and outstanding lodgements of £871. Assuming all other transactions are present, what is the balance of the Cash Book?

QUESTION 6

A business has received the following bank statement, enter any missing transactions and then balance the Cash Book.

Bank Statement				
Date	**Details**	**Debit**	**Credit**	**Balance**
01-11	Opening Balance			1,200.00 DR
03-11	Cheque 4356	456.00		1,656.00 DR
04-11	BACS Customer A		5,150.25	3,494.25 CR
08-11	BACS Customer B		2,400.50	5,894.75 CR
12-11	Rent	1100.00		4,794.75 CR
14-11	DD Electricity	275.00		4,519.75 CR
15-11	Cheque 4357	895.76		3,623.99 CR
17-11	Cheque 4358	766.40		2,857.59 CR
19-11	Bank charges	12.50		2,845.09 CR
24-11	BACS Customer C		1,899.86	4,744.95 CR

Cash Book - Bank					
Date	**Details**	**Amount**	**Date**	**Details**	**Amount**
04-11	BACS Customer A	5,150.25	01-11	Balance b/f	1,656,00
08-11	BACS Customer B	2,400.50	13-11	Cheque 4357	895.76
			15-11	Cheque 4358	766.40

QUESTION 7

Correctly categorise the following transactions.

	Outstanding Lodgement	Unpresented cheque
A cheque paid out recorded in the Cash Book but not yet showing on the bank statement.		
Money received from a credit customer showing in the Cash Book but not yet showing on the bank statement.		

QUESTION 8

A business has received the following bank statement, enter any missing transactions and then balance the Cash Book.

Bank Statement				
Date	Details	Debit	Credit	Balance
01-04	Opening Balance			1,350.00 CR
04-04	BACS Customer A		234.32	1,584.32 CR
08-04	Bank charges	7.00		1,577.32 CR
08-04	Bank Interest		1.35	1,578.67 CR
12-04	Cheque 234	42.83		1,535.84 CR
16-04	BACS Customer B		711.22	2,247.06 CR
19-04	Cheque 235	998.64		1,248.42 CR
22-04	DD - Rent	1320.00		71.58 DR
28-04	BACS Customer D		850.45	778.87 CR
30-04	Royal Office Ltd	95.00		683.87 CR

Cash Book - Bank					
Date	Details	Amount	Date	Details	Amount
01-04	Balance b/f	1,350.00	11-04	Cheque 234	42.83
05-04	BACS Customer A	234.32	18-04	Cheque 235	998.64
17-04	BACS Customer B	711.22	22-04	Rent	1320.00
29-04	BACS Customer C	476.54	30-04	Cheque 236	231.66

Complete the Bank Reconciliation Statement

Closing balance as per bank statement	
Add: outstanding lodgements	
Less: unpresented cheques	
Closing balance as per Cash Book	

This section has been created for you should you wish to use it to make notes or for calculations.

Skills & Knowledge Test — Chapter 2

QUESTION 10

Which is correct? (*tick the correct box*)

The journal is a double-entry account.	
The journal is the book of prime entry for non-regular transactions.	

QUESTION 11

Which of the following are non-regular transactions to be recorded in the journal?

Irrecoverable debts	
Payment of insurance premium	
Payroll transactions	
Opening entries for a business	
Money received from credit customer	
Correction of errors	
Money paid to credit supplier	

QUESTION 12

The following opening balances require entering in the accounting software as a journal entry. The figure for capital is missing and should be the balancing figure. You should also enter an appropriate narrative. Entries should be entered as single balances, not double-entry.

Bank (cash at bank)	£12,820
VAT (owed to HMRC)	£2,611
Fixtures and Fittings - at cost	£1,886
Bank Loan	£4,500
Purchases	£874
Cash	£236

Journal entry		Date: 01-04-2023	
Narrative:			
Account:		**Debit £**	**Credit £**
Capital			
	Totals:		

QUESTION 13

The following opening transactions require entering in the accounting software as a journal entry. You should also enter an appropriate narrative. Entries should be entered as double-entry transactions.

Transaction 1: £35,000 of Capital introduced into the business.

Transaction 2: £10,000 taken out as a bank loan.

Transaction 3: £6,750 spent on machinery (no VAT).

Journal entry		Date: 01-03-2023	
Narrative:			
Account:		**Debit £**	**Credit £**
	Totals:		

QUESTION 14

A customer, Company F, has ceased trading owing £175.00 + VAT. Complete the journal entry to write off the debt in the General Ledger and make the correct entry in the Receivables Ledger.

Journal entry:	Date: 14-01-2022	
Narrative:		
Account:	**Debit £**	**Credit £**

Receivables Ledger

Debit £	Credit £

QUESTION 15

A second customer, Company G, has ceased trading owing £246.00 excluding VAT. Complete the journal entry to write off the debt in the General Ledger and make the correct entry in the Receivables Ledger.

Journal entry:	Date: 16-01-2022	
Narrative:		
Account:	**Debit £**	**Credit £**

Receivables Ledger

Debit £	Credit £

This section has been created for you should you wish to use it to make notes or for calculations.

Skills & Knowledge Test — Chapter 3

QUESTION 16

Payroll transactions are non-regular transaction that involves the use of the journal. True or false?

True	
False	

QUESTION 17

Which amounts form part of the liability to HMRC?

Employer NI	
Employer Pension Contributions	
Employee NI	
Employee Pension Contributions	
Income Tax	
Trade Union Fees	
Charitable Donations	

QUESTION 18

Which of the following comprises the wages expense

Net wages + employer NI + employer pension contributions	
Gross wages + employer NI + employer pension contributions	
Gross wages + employee NI + employee pension contributions	
Net wages + employee NI + employee pension contributions	

QUESTION 19

A business has the following calculations for a monthly wage total. Enter the correct bookkeeping transactions into the accounts.

Wages Expense   £9,750
Income Tax   £1,866
Employer NI   £877
Employee NI   £748
Employer Pension   £650
Employee Pension   £650
Charitable Donations   £400

Wages Expense

Account	Amount £	Debit	Credit

Net Wages

Account	Amount £	Debit	Credit

HMRC

Account	Amount £	Debit	Credit

Pension Fund

Account	Amount £	Debit	Credit

Charitable Donations

Account	Amount £	Debit	Credit

QUESTION 20

A business has the following calculations for a monthly wage total. Enter the correct bookkeeping transactions into the accounts.

Gross Wages   £12,225
Income Tax   £2,143
Employer NI   £950
Employee NI   £920
Employer Pension   £710
Employee Pension   £700
Trade Union Fees   £250

Wages Expense

Account	Amount £	Debit	Credit

Net Wages

Account	Amount £	Debit	Credit

HMRC

Account	Amount £	Debit	Credit

Pension Fund

Account	Amount £	Debit	Credit

Trade Union Fees

Account	Amount £	Debit	Credit

This section has been created for you should you wish to use it to make notes or for calculations.

Skills & Knowledge Test — Chapter 4

QUESTION 21

Assign the following General Ledger Account balances to the correct sides of the trial balance and then calculate the two totals.

Trial Balance			
	Balance	Debit £	Credit £
Fixtures and Fittings	15,275		
Motor vehicles	25,940		
Bank (overdrawn)	11,236		
Petty Cash	127		
Receivables Ledger Control Account	9,834		
Payables Ledger Control Account	2,784		
Capital	9,765		
Drawings	4,675		
Sales	56,982		
Sales Returns	3,498		
Purchases	24,312		
Purchases Returns	1,098		
Discounts Allowed	786		
Discounts Received	911		
Rent Received	2,466		
Wages	7,833		
Travel Expenses	1,344		
Office Expenses	5,100		
VAT (owing to HMRC)	13,482		
	Total		

QUESTION 22

Assign the following General Ledger Account balances to the correct sides of the trial balance and then calculate the two totals.

In this case you will need to calculate the balance of the Capital Account based on the other information you have been given.

Trial Balance			
	Balance	Debit £	Credit £
Fixtures and Fittings	7,845		
Inventory	12,300		
Bank (cash at bank)	9,842		
Petty Cash	75		
Receivables Ledger Control Account	21,390		
Payables Ledger Control Account	6,529		
Capital			
Drawings	2,361		
Sales	45,900		
Sales Returns	1,462		
Purchases	18,750		
Purchases Returns	1,000		
Discounts Allowed	254		
Discounts Received	167		
Rent Paid	2,100		
Wages	9,016		
Electricity	4,355		
Office Expenses	1,200		
VAT (owing from HMRC)	1,788		
	Total		

QUESTION 23

Assign the following General Ledger Account balances to the correct sides of the trial balance and then calculate the two totals.

The Purchases Account has not yet been totalled and balanced.

Purchases Account			
Details	**Debit £**	**Details**	**Credit £**
Bank	1,463		
Bank	274		

Trial Balance			
	Balance	**Debit £**	**Credit £**
Inventory	4,300		
Motor vehicles	5,870		
Bank (overdrawn)	1,542		
Petty Cash	54		
Receivables Ledger Control Account	11,893		
Payables Ledger Control Account	4,552		
Capital	11,335		
Drawings	2,188		
Sales	13,452		
Sales Returns	544		
Purchases			
Purchases Returns	23		
Discounts Allowed	98		
Discounts Received	104		
Rent Paid	3,200		
Wages	4,700		
Travel Expenses	985		
Office Expenses	572		
VAT (owing to HMRC)	5,133		
Total			

This section has been created for you should you wish to use it to make notes or for calculations.

Skills & Knowledge Test – Chapter 5

QUESTION 24

Place the following transactions/totals on the correct sides of the VAT Control Account.

	Debit	Credit
VAT on sales		
VAT on purchases		
VAT on cash sales		
VAT on cash purchases		
VAT on discounts received		
VAT on discounts allowed		
VAT on sales returns		
VAT on purchases returns		
VAT paid to HMRC		
VAT refund received from HMRC		

QUESTION 25

A debit balance on the VAT Control Account will indicate that money is due to be paid to HMRC.

True	
False	

QUESTION 26

A credit balance on the VAT Control Account will indicate that money is due to be received from HMRC.

True	
False	

QUESTION 27

Complete then balance the VAT Control Account from the following totals. Dates are not required.

Details	Debit £	Details	Credit £

Note: these are totals of VAT and not net or gross totals.

Credit balance b/f	£9,865
Sales	£11,250
Purchases	£8,133
Sales Returns	£788
Purchases Returns	£128
Payment to HMRC	£9,865
Discounts Received	£321
Discounts Allowed	£486

The VAT return shows that £2,292 is due as a refund from HMRC. Does the VAT Control Account agree with this summary?

Yes	
No	

QUESTION 28

You have the following customer balances for the Receivables Ledger Control Account. What is the figure for the closing balance? (the £ symbol is not required)

Balance b/f	£12,563
Credit sales	£25,788
Sales Returns	£4,132
Money received	£28,411
Irrecoverable Debts	£1,897

QUESTION 29

The balance of the Receivables Ledger is £4,013. Using your number from the previous question (28), what could be the reason for an error in the Receivables Ledger? Identify any possible reasons.

Invoice has been omitted from the Receivables Ledger	
Invoice has been entered twice in the Receivables Ledger	
Credit Note has been understated in the Receivables Ledger	
Credit Note has been overstated in the Receivables Ledger	
Discounts Allowed has been omitted from the Receivables Ledger	
Discounts Allowed has been entered twice in the Receivables Ledger	

QUESTION 30

The balance of the Receivables Ledger is £25,216, and the balance of the Receivables Ledger Control Account is £23,998. Presuming the Receivables Ledger is correct, what could explain the error in the Receivables Ledger Control Account? Identify any possible reasons.

Invoice has been understated in the RLCA	
Invoice has been overstated in the RLCA	
Payment received has been omitted in the RLCA	
Payment received has been entered twice in the RLCA	
Irrecoverable Debts has been omitted in the RLCA	
Irrecoverable Debts has been entered twice in the RLCA	

QUESTION 31

Complete the Receivables Ledger Control and balance it, using the following known balances:

Balance b/f	£274
Sales made to credit customers	£1,567
Payments received from credit customers	£822
Dishonoured cheques	£135
Irrecoverable debts	£561
Contra	£35

Receivables Ledger Control Account			
Details	Debit £	Details	Credit £

QUESTION 32

A credit customer, Company F, has gone out of business, owing £280 + VAT. Enter the transaction to record the irrecoverable debt into the General Ledger

Account	Amount	Debit	Credit

What will be the entry in the Receivables Ledger?

Account	Amount	Debit	Credit

QUESTION 33

You have the following supplier balances for the Payables Ledger Control Account. What is the figure for the closing balance? (the £ symbol is not required)

Balance b/f	£21,898
Credit purchases	£41,261
Purchases Returns	£2,788
Payments made	£35,432

QUESTION 34

The balance of the Payables Ledger is £24,800. Using your number from the previous question (33), what could be the reason for the error in the Payables Ledger Control Account? Identify any possible reasons.

Invoice has been omitted from the PLCA	
Invoice has been entered twice in the PLCA	
Credit Note has been understated in the PLCA	
Credit Note has been overstated in the PLCA	
Discounts Received has been omitted from the PLCA	
Discounts Received has been entered twice in the PLCA	

QUESTION 35

The balance of the Payables Ledger is £32,984, and the balance of the Payables Ledger Control Account is £31,867. Presuming the Payables Ledger is correct, what could explain the error in the Payables Ledger Control Account? Identify any possible reasons.

Invoice has been understated in the PLCA	
Invoice has been overstated in the PLCA	
Payment received has been omitted in the PLCA	
Payment received has been entered twice in the PLCA	

QUESTION 36

Complete the Payables Ledger Control and balance it, using the following known balances:

Balance b/f	£896
Purchases made from credit suppliers	£2,133
Payments made to credit suppliers	£1,275
Contra	£35

Payables Ledger Control Account			
Details	Debit £	Details	Credit £

This section has been created for you should you wish to use it to make notes or for calculations.

Skills & Knowledge Test – Chapter 6

QUESTION 37

For each of the following errors that do not show up in the trial balance, identify the error.

Description	Error
Two errors have been made on different sides of the trial balance that cancel each other out.	
A transaction has not been entered into the accounting records.	
A transaction has been entered into the wrong expense account.	
A transaction has been entered into the wrong type of account.	
The same wrong numbers have been entered into the right sides of both accounts.	
The right numbers have been entered into the accounts, but on the wrong side of both accounts.	

QUESTION 38

A sales return for £57.00 excluding VAT to Company A has been left out of the accounting records. What will be the double-entry in the General Ledger and the Receivables Ledger to correct this error.

General Ledger

Account	Amount £	Debit	Credit

Receivables Ledger

Account	Amount £	Debit	Credit

QUESTION 39

A payment for telephone expenses of £90 (VAT not applicable) has been entered on the wrong side of both accounts.

What is the double-entry to remove the error?

Account	Amount £	Debit	Credit

What is the double-entry to correct the error?

Account	Amount £	Debit	Credit

QUESTION 40

Vehicle expenses for £45 (VAT not applicable) have been entered incorrectly in the Vehicles - At Cost Account.

What is the double-entry to remove the error?

Account	Amount £	Debit	Credit

QUESTION 41

A payment of £108 (VAT not applicable) for insurance has instead been entered in the accounts as a payment of £180.

What is the double-entry to remove the error?

Account	Amount £	Debit	Credit

What is the double-entry to correct the error?

Account	Amount £	Debit	Credit

QUESTION 42

A receipt of rent for £250 (VAT not applicable) has been recorded on the wrong side of both accounts.

What is the double-entry to remove the error?

Account	Amount £	Debit	Credit

What is the double-entry to correct the error?

Account	Amount £	Debit	Credit

QUESTION 43

A payment for office stationery of £56 (VAT not applicable) has been recorded in the bank account only.

What is the double-entry to correct the error?

Account	Amount £	Debit	Credit

QUESTION 44

A receipt for a cash sale of £186 has been recorded correctly in the Bank Account but as £168 in the Sales Account.

What is the double-entry to remove the error?

Account	Amount £	Debit	Credit

What is the double-entry to correct the error?

Account	Amount £	Debit	Credit

QUESTION 45

The balance of the Purchases Account has been underbalanced by £100.

What is the double-entry to correct the error?

Account	Amount £	Debit	Credit

QUESTION 46

A trial balance has been extracted, with debit entries of £95,267 and credit entries of £96,898. What entry will be required in the Suspense Account in order to balance the trial balance?

Account	Amount £	Debit	Credit

Once the errors have been investigated, it has been discovered that the following errors were present: (the other half of the double-entry was correct)

- A cash sale for £1,281 had been recorded twice in the Sales Account.
- Telephone expenses for £350 had been omitted from the Telephone Account.

What is the double-entry to remove the error in the Sales Account?

Account	Amount £	Debit	Credit

What is the double-entry to correct the error in the Telephone Account?

Account	Amount £	Debit	Credit

Complete the trial balance below. The amounts given are before correction. For the corrected accounts, take into consideration the corrections above.

Trial Balance			
Account	**Amount**	**Debit**	**Credit**
Vehicles at Cost	24,680		
Office Equipment At Cost	11,450		
Bank (Overdrawn)	9,056		
Cash	5,623		
Petty Cash	130		
Receivables Ledger Control Account	27,953		
Payables Ledger Control Account	18,247		
Capital	30,851		
Sales	38,744		
Purchases	22,948		
Telephone	2,483		
	Totals		

This section has been created for you should you wish to use it to make notes or for calculations.

Answers

Skills & Knowledge Test – Chapter 1

QUESTION 1

For each of the payment methods listed below, identify how long it will take for the transaction to be deducted from the bank account balance.

Method	Same Day	Next Day	At a later date when bill is paid
Cheque		✓	
Bank Draft	✓		
CHAPS	✓		
Cash	✓		
Credit card			✓
Standing order	✓		
Direct debit	✓		
Faster Payments	✓		
BACS	✓		
Debit card		✓	

QUESTION 2

For the following potential uses, match the transaction with the payment method. In your answer, enter the relevant number.

1 – a large purchase, e.g., property.

2 – expenses for travelling members of staff, e.g., salespersons.

3 – for buying tea and coffee from a local corner shop.

4 – purchase of a ream of printer paper online.

5 – paying a bill by post.

6 – buying a vehicle for the business.

7 – monthly payments of the same amount.

8 – monthly payments of varying amounts.

9 – payment of wages.

10 – paying a contractor's bill online.

Method	Potential purchase/expense
Cheque	5
Bank draft	6
CHAPS	1
Cash	3
Credit card	2
Standing order	7
Direct debit	8
Faster payments	10
BACS	9
Debit card	4

QUESTION 3

Highlight each of the following actions that will improve the solvency of a business, by either keeping cash in the business for longer or by maximising the speed of incoming cash.

Action	Will improve solvency
Pay by cheque whenever possible	
Encourage customers to pay by cheque	
Pay suppliers as soon as possible	
Pay suppliers as late as possible (within the terms)	✓
Encourage customers to pay as late as possible (within the terms)	
Encourage customers to pay as soon as possible by offering discounts	✓

QUESTION 4

The balance of the bank account on the bank statement is £4,522 CR. The Cash Book shows unpresented cheques of £980 and outstanding lodgements of £1,210. Assuming all other transactions are present, what is the balance of the Cash Book?

```
4,752 (debit)
```

(4,522 - 980 + 1210)

QUESTION 5

The balance of the bank account on the bank statement is £466 DR. The Cash Book shows unpresented cheques of £234 and outstanding lodgements of £871. Assuming all other transactions are present, what is the balance of the Cash Book?

```
171 (debit)
```

(466 overdrawn - 234 + 871)

QUESTION 6

A business has received the following bank statement, enter any missing transactions and then balance the Cash Book.

Bank Statement				
Date	Details	Debit	Credit	Balance
01-11	Opening Balance			1,200.00 DR
03-11	Cheque 4356	456.00		1,656.00 DR
04-11	BACS Customer A		5,150.25	3,494.25 CR
08-11	BACS Customer B		2,400.50	5,894.75 CR
12-11	Rent	1100.00		4,794.75 CR
14-11	DD Electricity	275.00		4,519.75 CR
15-11	Cheque 4357	895.76		3,623.99 CR
17-11	Cheque 4358	766.40		2,857.59 CR
19-11	Bank charges	12.50		2,845.09 CR
24-11	BACS Customer C		1,899.86	4,744.95 CR

Cash Book - Bank					
Date	Details	Amount	Date	Details	Amount
04-11	BACS Customer A	5,150.25	01-11	Balance b/f	1,656,00
08-11	BACS Customer B	2,400.50	13-11	Cheque 4357	895.76
24-11	BACS Customer C	1,899.86	15-11	Cheque 4358	766.40
			12-11	Rent	1,100.00
			14-11	DD Electricity	275.00
			19-11	Bank charges	12.50
			30-11	Balance c/d	4,744.95
		9,450.61			9,450.61
01-12	Balance b/d	4,744.95			

QUESTION 7

Correctly categorise the following transactions.

	Outstanding Lodgement	Unpresented cheque
A cheque paid out recorded in the Cash Book but not yet showing on the bank statement.		✓
Money received from a credit customer showing in the Cash Book but not yet showing on the bank statement.	✓	

QUESTION 8

A business has received the following bank statement, enter any missing transactions and then balance the Cash Book.

Bank Statement				
Date	Details	Debit	Credit	Balance
01-04	Opening Balance			1,350.00 CR
04-04	BACS Customer A		234.32	1,584.32 CR
08-04	Bank charges	7.00		1,577.32 CR
08-04	Bank Interest		1.35	1,578.67 CR
12-04	Cheque 234	42.83		1,535.84 CR
16-04	BACS Customer B		711.22	2,247.06 CR
19-04	Cheque 235	998.64		1,248.42 CR
22-04	DD - Rent	1320.00		71.58 DR
28-04	BACS Customer D		850.45	778.87 CR
30-04	Royal Office Ltd	95.00		683.87 CR

Cash Book - Bank						
Date	Details	Amount	Date	Details	Amount	
01-04	Balance b/f	1,350.00	11-04	Cheque 234	42.83	
05-04	BACS Customer A	234.32	18-04	Cheque 235	998.64	
17-04	BACS Customer B	711.22	22-04	Rent	1320.00	
29-04	BACS Customer C	476.54	30-04	Cheque 236	231.66	
08-04	Bank Interest	1.35	08-04	Bank charges	7.00	
28-04	BACS Customer D	850.45	30-04	Royal Office Ltd	95.00	
			30-04	Balance c/d	928.75	
		3,623.88			3,623.88	
01-05		928.75				

Complete the Bank Reconciliation Statement

Closing balance as per bank statement	683.87
Add: outstanding lodgements	
BACS Customer C	476.54
	476.64
Less: unpresented cheques	
Cheque 236	231.66
	231.66
Closing balance as per Cash Book	928.75

Skills & Knowledge Test — Chapter 2

QUESTION 10

Which is correct? (*tick the correct box*)

The journal is a double-entry account.	
The journal is the book of prime entry for non-regular transactions.	✓

QUESTION 11

Which of the following are non-regular transactions to be recorded in the journal?

Irrecoverable debts	✓
Payment of insurance premium	
Payroll transactions	✓
Opening entries for a business	✓
Money received from credit customer	
Correction of errors	✓
Money paid to credit supplier	

QUESTION 12

The following opening balances require entering in the accounting software as a journal entry. The figure for capital is missing and should be the balancing figure. You should also enter an appropriate narrative. Entries should be entered as single balances, not double-entry.

Bank (cash at bank)	£12,820
VAT (owed to HMRC)	£2,611
Fixtures and Fittings - at cost	£1,886
Bank Loan	£4,500
Purchases	£874
Cash	£236

Journal entry	Date: 01-04-2023	
Narrative:		

Account:	Debit £	Credit £
Bank	12,820	
VAT (owed to HMRC)		2,611
Fixtures and Fittings - at cost	1,886	
Bank Loan		4,500
Purchases	874	
Cash	236	
Capital		8,705
Totals:	15,816	15,816

QUESTION 13

The following opening transactions require entering in the accounting software as a journal entry. You should also enter an appropriate narrative. Entries should be entered as double-entry transactions.

Transaction 1: £35,000 of Capital introduced into the business.

Transaction 2: £10,000 taken out as a bank loan.

Transaction 3: £6,750 spent on machinery (no VAT).

Journal entry	Date: 01-03-2023	
Narrative:		

Account:	Debit £	Credit £
Bank	35,000	
Capital		35,000
Bank	10,000	
Bank Loan		10,000
Machinery - at cost	6,750	
Bank		6,750
Totals:	51,750	51,750

QUESTION 14

A customer, Company F, has ceased trading owing £175.00 + VAT. Complete the journal entry to write off the debt in the General Ledger and make the correct entry in the Receivables Ledger.

Journal entry:	Date: 14-01-2022	
Narrative: writing off irrecoverable debt for Company F		
Account:	**Debit £**	**Credit £**
Irrecoverable Debts	175.00	
VAT	35.00	
Receivables Ledger Control Account		210.00

Receivables Ledger

Company F		
Debit £		Credit £
	Journal*	210.00

*students will not be asked to add this detail in an assessment.

QUESTION 15

A second customer, Company G, has ceased trading owing £246.00 including VAT. Complete the journal entry to write off the debt in the General Ledger and make the correct entry in the Receivables Ledger.

Journal entry:	Date: 16-01-2022	
Narrative: writing off irrecoverable debt for Company G		
Account:	**Debit £**	**Credit £**
Irrecoverable Debts	246.00	
VAT	49.20	
Receivables Ledger Control Account		295.20

Receivables Ledger

Debit £		Credit £
	Journal*	295.20

*students will not be asked to add this detail in an assessment.

Skills & Knowledge Test – Chapter 3

QUESTION 16

Payroll transactions are non-regular transaction that involves the use of the journal. True or false?

True	✓
False	

QUESTION 17

Which amounts form part of the liability to HMRC?

Employer NI	✓
Employer Pension Contributions	
Employee NI	✓
Employee Pension Contributions	
Income Tax	✓
Trade Union Fees	
Charitable Donations	

QUESTION 18

Which of the following comprises the wages expense

Net wages + employer NI + employer pension contributions	
Gross wages + employer NI + employer pension contributions	✓
Gross wages + employee NI + employee pension contributions	
Net wages + employee NI + employee pension contributions	

QUESTION 19

A business has the following calculations for a monthly wage total. Enter the correct bookkeeping transactions into the accounts.

Wages Expense	£9,750
Income Tax	£1,866
Employer NI	£877
Employee NI	£748
Employer Pension	£650
Employee Pension	£650
Charitable Donations	£400

Wages Expense

Account	Amount £	Debit	Credit
Wages Expense	9,750	✓	
Wages Control	9,750		✓

Net Wages

Account	Amount £	Debit	Credit
Wages Control	4,559	✓	
Bank	4,559		✓

HMRC

Account	Amount £	Debit	Credit
Wages Control	3,491	✓	
HMRC	3,491		✓

Pension Fund

Account	Amount £	Debit	Credit
Wages Control	1,300	✓	
Pension Fund	1,300		✓

Charitable Donations

Account	Amount £	Debit	Credit
Wages Control	400	✓	
Charitable Donations	400		✓

QUESTION 20

A business has the following calculations for a monthly wage total. Enter the correct bookkeeping transactions into the accounts.

Gross Wages	£12,225
Income Tax	£2,143
Employer NI	£950
Employee NI	£920
Employer Pension	£710
Employee Pension	£700
Trade Union Fees	£250

Wages Expense

Account	Amount £	Debit	Credit
Wages Expense	13,885	✓	
Wages Control	13,885		✓

Net Wages

Account	Amount £	Debit	Credit
Wages Control	8,212	✓	
Bank	8,212		✓

HMRC

Account	Amount £	Debit	Credit
Wages Control	4,013	✓	
HMRC	4,013		✓

Pension Fund

Account	Amount £	Debit	Credit
Wages Control	1,410	✓	
Pension	1,410		✓

Trade Union Fees

Account	Amount £	Debit	Credit
Wages Control	250	✓	
Trade Union	250		✓

Skills & Knowledge Test — Chapter 4

QUESTION 21

Assign the following General Ledger Account balances to the correct sides of the trial balance and then calculate the two totals.

Trial Balance	Balance	Debit £	Credit £
Fixtures and Fittings	15,275	15,275	
Motor vehicles	25,940	25,940	
Bank (overdrawn)	11,236		11,236
Petty Cash	127	127	
Receivables Ledger Control Account	9,834	9,834	
Payables Ledger Control Account	2,784		2,784
Capital	9,765		9,765
Drawings	4,675	4,675	
Sales	56,982		56,982
Sales Returns	3,498	3,498	
Purchases	24,312	24,312	
Purchases Returns	1,098		1,098
Discounts Allowed	786	786	
Discounts Received	911		911
Rent Received	2,466		2,466
Wages	7,833	7,833	
Travel Expenses	1,344	1,344	
Office Expenses	5,100	5,100	
VAT (owing to HMRC)	13,482		13,482
Total		98,274	98,274

QUESTION 22

Assign the following General Ledger Account balances to the correct sides of the trial balance and then calculate the two totals.

In this case you will need to calculate the balance of the Capital Account based on the other information you have been given.

Trial Balance			
	Balance	Debit £	Credit £
Fixtures and Fittings	7,845	7,845	
Inventory	12,300	12,300	
Bank (cash at bank)	9,842	9,842	
Petty Cash	75	75	
Receivables Ledger Control Account	21,390	21,390	
Payables Ledger Control Account	6,529		6,529
Capital			39,142
Drawings	2,361	2,361	
Sales	45,900		45,900
Sales Returns	1,462	1,462	
Purchases	18,750	18,750	
Purchases Returns	1,000		1,000
Discounts Allowed	254	254	
Discounts Received	167		167
Rent Paid	2,100	2,100	
Wages	9,016	9,016	
Electricity	4,355	4,355	
Office Expenses	1,200	1,200	
VAT (owing from HMRC)	1,788	1,788	
	Total	92,738	92,738

QUESTION 23

Assign the following General Ledger Account balances to the correct sides of the trial balance and then calculate the two totals.

The Purchases Account has not yet been totalled and balanced.

Purchases Account			
Details	Debit £	Details	Credit £
Bank	1,463	Balance c/d	1,737
Bank	274		
	1,737		1,737
Balance b/d	1,737		

Trial Balance			
	Balance	Debit £	Credit £
Inventory	4,300	4,300	
Motor vehicles	5,870	5,870	
Bank (overdrawn)	1,542		1,542
Petty Cash	54	54	
Receivables Ledger Control Account	11,893	11,893	
Payables Ledger Control Account	4,552		4,552
Capital	11,335		11,335
Drawings	2,188	2,188	
Sales	13,452		13,452
Sales Returns	544	544	
Purchases	1,737	1,737	
Purchases Returns	23		23
Discounts Allowed	98	98	
Discounts Received	104		104
Rent Paid	3,200	3,200	
Wages	4,700	4,700	
Travel Expenses	985	985	
Office Expenses	572	572	
VAT (owing to HMRC)	5,133		5,133
	Total	36,141	36,141

Skills & Knowledge Test – Chapter 5

QUESTION 24

Place the following transactions/totals on the correct sides of the VAT Control Account.

	Debit	Credit
VAT on sales		✓
VAT on purchases	✓	
VAT on cash sales		✓
VAT on cash purchases	✓	
VAT on discounts received		✓
VAT on discounts allowed	✓	
VAT on sales returns	✓	
VAT on purchases returns		✓
VAT paid to HMRC	✓	
VAT refund received from HMRC		✓

QUESTION 25

A debit balance on the VAT Control Account will indicate that money is due to be paid to HMRC.

True	
False	✓

QUESTION 26

A credit balance on the VAT Control Account will indicate that money is due to be received from HMRC.

True	
False	✓

QUESTION 27

Complete then balance the VAT Control Account from the following totals. Dates are not required.

VAT Control Account			
Details	**Debit £**	**Details**	**Credit £**
Purchases	8,133	Balance b/f	9,865
Sales Returns	788	Sales	11,250
Payment to HMRC	9,865	Purchases Returns	128
Discounts Allowed	486	Discounts Received	321
Balance c/d	2,292		
	21,564		21,564
		Balance b/d	2,292

Note: these are totals of VAT and not net or gross totals.

Credit balance b/f	£9,865
Sales	£11.250
Purchases	£8,133
Sales Returns	£788
Purchases Returns	£128
Payment to HMRC	£9.865
Discounts Received	£321
Discounts Allowed	£486

The VAT return shows that £2,292 is due as a refund from HMRC. Does the VAT Control Account agree with this summary?

Yes	
No	✓

QUESTION 28

You have the following customer balances for the Receivables Ledger Control Account. What is the figure for the closing balance? (the £ symbol is not required)

Balance b/f	£12,563
Credit sales	£25,788
Sales Returns	£4,132
Money received	£28,411
Irrecoverable Debts	£1,897

3,911

QUESTION 29

The balance of the Receivables Ledger is £4,013. Using your number from the previous question (28), what could be the reason for an error in the Receivables Ledger? Identify any possible reasons.

Invoice has been omitted from the Receivables Ledger	
Invoice has been entered twice in the Receivables Ledger	✓
Credit Note has been understated in the Receivables Ledger	✓
Credit Note has been overstated in the Receivables Ledger	
Discounts Allowed has been omitted from the Receivables Ledger	✓
Discounts Allowed has been entered twice in the Receivables Ledger	

QUESTION 30

The balance of the Receivables Ledger is £25,216, and the balance of the Receivables Ledger Control Account is £23,998. Presuming the Receivables Ledger is correct, what could explain the error in the Receivables Ledger Control Account? Identify any possible reasons.

Invoice has been understated in the RLCA	✓
Invoice has been overstated in the RLCA	
Payment received has been omitted in the RLCA	
Payment received has been entered twice in the RLCA	✓
Irrecoverable Debts has been omitted in the RLCA	
Irrecoverable Debts has been entered twice in the RLCA	✓

QUESTION 31

Complete the Receivables Ledger Control and balance it, using the following known balances:

Balance b/f	£274
Sales made to credit customers	£1,567
Payments received from credit customers	£822
Dishonoured cheques	£135
Irrecoverable debts	£561
Contra	£35

Receivables Ledger Control Account				
Details	**Debit £**	**Details**		**Credit £**
Balance b/f	274	Bank		822
Sales	1,567	Contra		35
Dishonoured cheques	135	Irrecoverable debts		561
		Balance c/d		558
	1,976			1,976
Balance b/d	558			

QUESTION 32

A credit customer, Company F, has gone out of business, owing £280 + VAT. Enter the transaction to record the irrecoverable debt into the General Ledger.

Account	Amount	Debit	Credit
Irrecoverable Debts	280.00	✓	
VAT	56.00	✓	
Receivables Ledger Control Account	336.00		✓

What will be the entry in the Receivables Ledger?

Account	Amount	Debit	Credit
Company F	336.00		✓

QUESTION 33

You have the following supplier balances for the Payables Ledger Control Account. What is the figure for the closing balance? (the £ symbol is not required)

Balance b/f	£21,898
Credit purchases	£41,261
Purchases Returns	£2,788
Payments made	£35,432

24,939

QUESTION 34

The balance of the Payables Ledger is £24,800. Using your number from the previous question (33), what could be the reason for an error in the Payables Ledger? Identify any possible reasons.

Invoice has been omitted from the PLCA	✓
Invoice has been entered twice in the PLCA	
Credit Note has been understated in the PLCA	
Credit Note has been overstated in the PLCA	✓
Discounts Received has been omitted from the PLCA	
Discounts Received has been entered twice in the PLCA	✓

QUESTION 35

The balance of the Payables Ledger is £32,984, and the balance of the Payables Ledger Control Account is £31,867. Presuming the Payables Ledger is correct, what could explain an error in the Payables Ledger Control Account? Identify any possible reasons.

Invoice has been understated in the PLCA	✓
Invoice has been overstated in the PLCA	
Payment received has been omitted in the PLCA	
Payment received has been entered twice in the PLCA	✓

QUESTION 36

Complete the Payables Ledger Control and balance it, using the following known balances:

Balance b/f	£896
Purchases made from credit suppliers	£2,133
Payments made to credit suppliers	£1,275
Contra	£35

Payables Ledger Control Account			
Details	**Debit £**	**Details**	**Credit £**
Bank	1,275	Balance b/f	896
Contra	35	Purchases	2,133
Balance c/d	1,719		
	3,029		3,029
		Balance b/d	1,719

Skills & Knowledge Test – Chapter 6

QUESTION 37

For each of the following errors that do not show up in the trial balance, identify the error.

Description	Error
Two errors have been made on different sides of the trial balance that cancel each other out.	Compensating error
A transaction has not been entered into the accounting records.	Error of omission
A transaction has been entered into the wrong expense account.	Error of commission
A transaction has been entered into the wrong type of account.	Error of principle
The same wrong numbers have been entered into the right sides of both accounts.	Error or original entry
The right numbers have been entered into the accounts, but on the wrong side of both accounts.	Reversal of entries

QUESTION 38

A sales return for £57.00 excluding VAT to Company A has been left out of the accounting records. What will be the double-entry in the General Ledger and the Receivables Ledger to correct this error.

General Ledger

Account	Amount £	Debit	Credit
Sales	57.00		✓
VAT	11.40		✓
Receivables Ledger Control Account	68.40	✓	

Receivables Ledger

Account	Amount £	Debit	Credit
Company A	68.40	✓	

QUESTION 39

A payment for telephone expenses of £90 (VAT not applicable) has been entered on the wrong side of both accounts.

What is the double-entry to remove the error?

Account	Amount £	Debit	Credit
Telephone Expenses	90.00	✓	
Bank	90.00		✓

What is the double-entry to correct the error?

Account	Amount £	Debit	Credit
Telephone Expenses	90.00	✓	
Bank	90.00		✓

QUESTION 40

Vehicle expenses for £45 (VAT not applicable) have been entered incorrectly in the Vehicles - At Cost Account.

What is the double-entry to remove the error?

Account	Amount £	Debit	Credit
Vehicle Expenses	45.00	✓	
Vehicles - At Cost	45.00		✓

QUESTION 41

A payment of £108 (VAT not applicable) for insurance has instead been entered in the accounts as a payment of £180.

What is the double-entry to remove the error?

Account	Amount £	Debit	Credit
Bank	180.00	✓	
Insurance	180.00		✓

What is the double-entry to correct the error?

Account	Amount £	Debit	Credit
Insurance	108.00	✓	
Bank	108.00		✓

QUESTION 42

A receipt of rent for £250 (VAT not applicable) has been recorded on the wrong side of both accounts.

What is the double-entry to remove the error?

Account	Amount £	Debit	Credit
Rent Received	250.00		✓
Bank	250.00	✓	

What is the double-entry to correct the error?

Account	Amount £	Debit	Credit
Rent Received	250.00		✓
Bank	250.00	✓	

QUESTION 43

A payment for office stationery of £56 (VAT not applicable) has been recorded in the bank account only.

What is the double-entry to correct the error?

Account	Amount £	Debit	Credit
Office Stationery	56.00	✓	
Suspense	56.00		✓

QUESTION 44

A receipt for a cash sale of £186 has been recorded correctly in the Bank Account but as £168 in the Sales Account.

What is the double-entry to remove the error?

Account	Amount £	Debit	Credit
Sales	168.00	✓	
Suspense	168.00		✓

What is the double-entry to correct the error?

Account	Amount £	Debit	Credit
Suspense	186.00	✓	
Sales	186.00		✓

QUESTION 45

The balance of the Purchases Account has been underbalanced by £100.

What is the double-entry to correct the error?

Account	Amount £	Debit	Credit
Purchases	100.00	✓	
Suspense	100.00		✓

QUESTION 46

A trial balance has been extracted, with debit entries of £95,267 and credit entries of £96,198. What entry will be required in the Suspense Account in order to balance the trial balance?

Account	Amount £	Debit	Credit
Suspense	1,631.00	✓	

Once the errors have been investigated, it has been discovered that the following errors were present: (the other half of the double-entry was correct)

- A cash sale for £1,281 had been recorded twice in the Sales Account.
- Telephone expenses for £350 had been omitted from the Telephone Account.

What is the double-entry to remove the error in the Sales Account?

Account	Amount £	Debit	Credit
Sales	1,281.00	✓	
Suspense	1,281.00		✓

What is the double-entry to correct the error in the Telephone Account?

Account	Amount £	Debit	Credit
Telephone	350.00	✓	
Suspense	350.00		✓

Complete the trial balance below. The amounts given are before correction. For the corrected accounts, take into consideration the corrections above.

Trial Balance			
Account	Amount	Debit	Credit
Vehicles at Cost	24,680	24,680	
Office Equipment At Cost	11,450	11,450	
Bank (Overdrawn)	9,056		9,056
Cash	5,623	5,623	
Petty Cash	130	130	
Receivables Ledger Control Account	27,953	27,953	
Payables Ledger Control Account	18,247		18,247
Capital	30,851		30,851
Sales	38,744		37,463
Purchases	22,948	22,948	
Telephone	2,483	2,833	
	Totals	95,617	95,617

This section has been created for you should you wish to use it to make notes or for calculations.

Printed in Great Britain
by Amazon